Alkaline Smoothies

Lose Weight & Supercharge Your Health with Green Smoothies and Vegan Protein Smoothies

By Karen G. Love

Copyright ©Karen G. Love 2016

All rights reserved. No part of this publication may be reproduced, stored in a retrieval system, or transmitted, in any form or by any means, electronic, mechanical, photocopying, recording or otherwise, without the prior written permission of the author and the publishers.

The scanning, uploading, and distribution of this book via the Internet, or via any other means, without the permission of the author is illegal and punishable by law. Please purchase only authorized electronic editions, and do not participate in or encourage electronic piracy of copyrighted materials.

All information in this book has been carefully researched and checked for factual accuracy. However, the author and publishers make no warranty, expressed or implied, that the information contained herein is appropriate for every individual, situation or purpose, and assume no responsibility for errors or omission. The reader assumes the risk and full responsibility for all actions, and the author will not be held liable for any loss or damage, whether consequential, incidental, and special or otherwise, that may result from the information presented in this publication.

All cooking is an experiment in a sense, and many people come to the same or similar recipe over time. All recipes in this book have been derived from author's personal experience.

Should any bear a close resemblance to those used elsewhere, that is purely coincidental.

The book is not intended to provide medical advice or to take the place of medical advice and treatment from your personal physician. Readers are advised to consult their own doctors or other qualified health professionals regarding the treatment of medical conditions. The author shall not be held liable or responsible for any misunderstanding or misuse of the information contained in this book. The information is not intended to diagnose, treat or cure any disease.

It is important to remember that the author of this book is not a doctor/ medical professional. Only opinions based upon her own personal experiences or research are cited. THE AUTHOR DOES NOT OFFER MEDICAL ADVICE or prescribe any treatments. For any health or medical issues – you should be talking to your doctor first.

Contents

Chapter 1: Raw Foods and Green Drinks 14

    Other Unique Benefits of Eating Raw Foods................................18

Chapter 2: The Power of Superfoods 20

Chapter 3: 15 Delicious Breakfast Smoothies................................. 27

Chapter 4: Savory Meal Replacement Smoothies 38

Chapter 5: 14 Sweet Dessert Smoothies 56

Chapter 6: Creative and Unique Smoothie Ideas 68

Conclusion 86

Introduction

Thank you for taking an interest in this book. It really means a lot to me and I am looking forward to inspiring you and helping you restore vibrant health and, if desired lose weight, with amazing Alkaline Smoothies.

Did you know that more than two-thirds of Americans have tried dieting for weight loss and good health? Chances are you have already tried a diet plan, or two, and came to the conclusion that sticking to it was not giving you the results you really wanted. This is not a surprise, as people all over the world share this same story. There are literally hundreds of dieting programs and weight loss regiments that "guarantee" results in a matter of weeks, or even days. But, as you now know, the reality is that not all weight loss plans work. This is especially true for vegans and vegetarians, who are not usually taken into account with the mainstream health and

Introduction

wellness industry. While most diets are fads that come and go as often as the seasons, the alkaline diet is one that is here to stay.

Geared towards vegans and veggie lovers, the alkaline diet has quickly become one of the most efficient and effective modern weight loss plans today. The word alkaline may throw you off at first, as alkaline acid is found in batteries and sounds like it could possibly poison you if consumed. But the alkaline diet plan was formed around the theory of avoiding foods that increase the natural acids in your body. Foods like meat, refined sugar, wheat, and processed goods cause you to produce too much acid, which is bad for your body. But eating certain foods that make your body more alkaline can prevent your body from developing medical issues related to acids and help you lose weight.

Introduction

Let's break down the science behind this diet, so you can better understand how eating only plant-based foods helps to heal your body and promote wellness. A pH level determines how acidic or alkaline something is; in this case, we are measuring how acidic food is. A pH level of zero means that the food is completely acidic; and a pH level of fourteen is alkaline. This means that a measurement of seven is neutral. Your pH levels vary throughout the body. For example, blood is more alkaline, while the stomach is significantly acidic. Your urine's pH levels vary depending on what food you eat; it is how your body regulates the pH levels in your bloodstream. The alkaline diet helps your body regulate your blood pH levels.

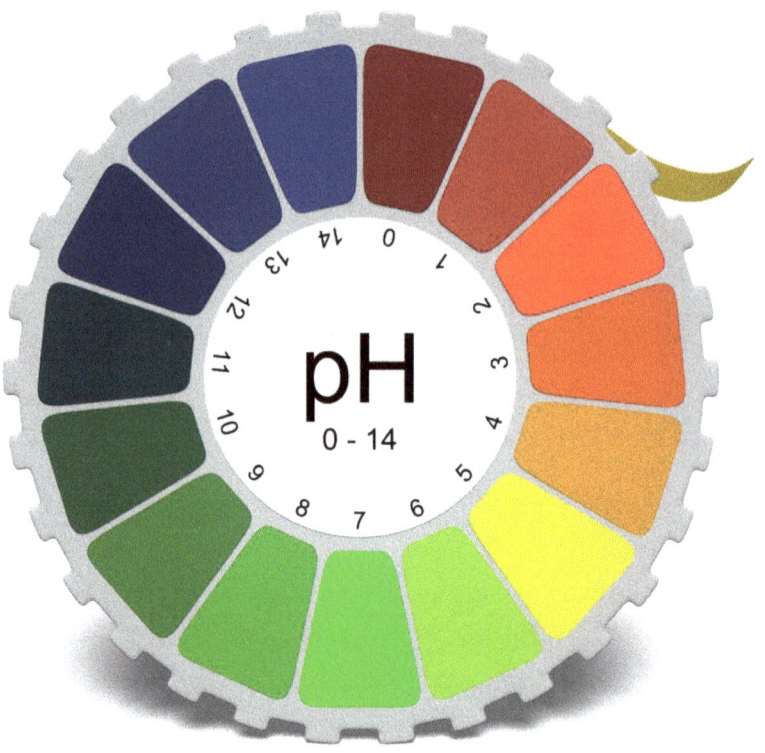

Not only do the foods that are recommended for the alkaline diet maintain a healthy pH balance throughout your entire body, they also support healthy weight loss, disease prevention, and a heightened immune system. While on the alkaline diet, try to consume a lot of organic fruits and vegetables, followed with at least eight glasses of water every day. This diet is the epitome of clean eating and organic living. And the resulting health benefits make this lifestyle change that much more appealing.

Introduction

The excess consumption of fruits and vegetables, paired with the reduced intake of animal protein and processed carbohydrates can truly change your life for the better. The alkaline diet will help prevent the development of kidney stones, strengthen muscles, increase bone density, improve health brain function, improve heart health, reduce the risk of developing cardiovascular disease, reduce lower back pain, lower your risk of developing type two diabetes, reduce gas and bloating, and improve the symptoms of arthritis.

Introduction

Just like any diet, there are obvious restrictions to this weight loss plan as well. The alkaline diet follows the methods of veganism closely, so most fruits and vegetables are the foundation to this lifestyle. But, you can also eat soy, tofu, nuts, seeds, legumes, and plant-based protein supplements. This means that simple sugars, meat, dairy, and processed food products should be eliminated (or at least drastically reduced).

You must also avoid consuming alcohol or caffeine. If you are a morning coffee drinker, this may put you off a bit. The population of individuals making it through the day without a caffeinated supplement is significantly small in comparison to the coffee drinkers of the world. But after just a few days on the alkaline diet, you will notice that your energy and mood will boost up and leave you with more energy, motivation, and focus than the short caffeine

Introduction

high coffee gives you. I know, this one is hard, but don't worry. You can transition to a caffeine-free lifestyle slowly, and as long as you eat clean and pretty alkaline, you can have coffee as a treat every now and then.

With so many rules and guidelines, it can be difficult to take on a new lifestyle and completely change your diet. However, having dozens of delicious and satisfying recipes will keep your tummy happy and aid weight loss. Smoothies have become one of the most popular dieting elements in recent years. But this isn't really a surprise; smoothies are fast and easy to make, only include three or four key ingredients, and have an endless amount of possible combinations. Not to mention, they are really filling, fulfill your veggie and fruit intake for the day, and often contain less calories than the meal you would usually have in its place (still, we do not need to torture ourselves with excessive calories counting on this lifestyle).

Introduction

In this book, you will learn everything you need to know about sticking to the alkaline diet by becoming a master at blending smoothies. Not only does this book contain over fifty unique and tasty smoothie recipes, but also a list of superfoods and how they improve your health, a guide to creating your own smoothies, a detailed explanation of how to best transition into the alkaline lifestyle, and so much more. While all the recipes are 100% vegan and fully compatible with a vegan plant-based lifestyle, I welcome you all. This book is not only for vegans and vegetarians.

I have included dozens of delicious smoothie recipes that will satisfy anyone's taste buds. From breakfast juices, to meal replacement drinks, to sweet dessert smoothies, there are almost too many combinations to try! Here is an inescapable fact: every fitness and health expert out there claims to have the secret to weight loss

Introduction

success. But very few of those methods actually work and don't explain how to still enjoy food while trying to lose weight. Smoothies can be sweet, savory, and adventurous in flavor, which keep your taste buds guessing and your stomach full. They only take minutes to make and will keep you from binging on tempting refined sugary goods later. Perfect for busy people. All you need is a blender (and some motivation, but if you have picked up this book you already are motivated and I am looking forward to sharing my passion for a healthy alkaline lifestyle with you).

It is time for you to become an expert of the alkaline diet and smoothies. The green and vegan recipes in this book are guaranteed to help you reach your nutrient goals, lose weight, and feel amazing.

Thanks again for taking an interest in this book; I hope that it will inspire you to never give up on your weight loss dreams and give you the success you deserve. Good luck on your health and wellness journey. Enjoy!

Introduction

Introduction

Are You Interested in Healthy, Vegan Friendly Recipes to Revolutionize Your Health?

If yes, join my free newsletter.

As a special gift, you will immediately receive a free complimentary PDF eBook with dozens of inspiring recipes to help you on your journey. Not to mention other bonuses, discounts on my new books, valuable freebies, and more inspiration delivered to your inbox. Don't worry about spam or annoying marketing emails, it's not my style.

Visit the link below to join our vegan health newsletter and get a free eBook now (it's exclusive to our subscribers only):

www.yourwellnessbooks.com/karen-smoothies

www.bitly.com/karenfreegift

Introduction

Any technical problems? Don't worry, we got you covered!

Just email me: karenveganbooks@gmail.com

Chapter 1: Raw Foods and Green Drinks

Now that you have made the decision to change your lifestyle, you have to learn everything you can about the alkaline diet and consuming more raw and organic foods. Raw foods are uncooked, unprocessed foods like fruits, vegetables, nuts and seeds. While the alkaline diet plan does suggest that you try to increase the amount of raw foods you consume, it does not mean that you cannot cook your vegetables or enjoy a hot meal. Personally, I like combining raw vegan food with cooked vegan food. However, it is crucial that you understand why consuming raw foods is beneficial for your health and how you can experience the amazing benefits of raw food.

The concept of eating raw foods is that heating food, whether in a pan, oven, or microwave, destroys all of the nutrient and natural enzymes that the food had. Not only does this make your body miss out on improving vitamin and nutrient deficiencies, but it also results in your body having trouble with digestion and fighting chronic disease.

Some individuals who regularly practice a raw food diet believe that cooking food makes it toxic, and that the cook is actually killing the food. Despite these assumptions and beliefs, consuming raw food has a few benefits of its own. Some of the many health benefits of eating raw food include: curing headaches, clearing up allergies, improving your memory, preventing and curing type two diabetes, boosting immunity, and improving your memory.

Although the alkaline diet plan seems simple enough, making the necessary changes to transition into a healthy lifestyle is much more difficult than what is believed. The Western diet thrives off of carbohydrates, oversized portions, and tons of meat. Most of the food in the grocery store is filled with refined sugars and processed ingredients that can cause serious health problems. The prime examples of uncooked, unprocessed, organic foods that you can enjoy on the alkaline diet are: fruits (especially fruits that are low in sugar such as limes, lemons, grapefruits, pomegranates-these are super alkaline even though they may taste a bit acidic), vegetables, nuts, seeds, and sprouted grains. Unfortunately, anything that was not mentioned is off limits the entire time you are living an alkaline lifestyle. This means that meat, eggs, dairy, fish, bread, candy, desserts, and any other type of processed, heavy food is a part of the "do not eat" category.

Although cooking food may be off limits most of the time on the alkaline diet, you do have other options to help you prepare your meals. You can use blenders, dehydrators, and food processors to prepare your meals. As long as the fruits and veggies do not go above 118 degrees Fahrenheit in temperature, (40-45 Celsius) then you are in the clear.

It is always suggested that pregnant women, young children, senior citizen, individuals with weakened immune systems, and persons with chronic medical conditions do not participate in a raw food diet or the alkaline weight loss plan. Therefore, you should absolutely speak with your healthcare provider prior to starting any new lifestyle changes or diet plans.

While eating a primarily raw food diet, you will most likely unintentionally lose weight, as most vegetables and fruits contain a small amount of calories and fat, while they remain high in fiber. However, to truly experience the amazing benefits of a raw food diet, you must ensure that your meals contain all of the essential nutrients that your body needs to function. It can be difficult to supplement protein into your diet with plant- based ingredients, as well are iron, vitamin B12, and calcium. Therefore, you must take care to find foods that are high in these nutrients, which we will later discuss in Chapter 2.

Other incredible health benefits of a raw food plan include:

- reduced inflammation
- improved digestion
- more dietary fiber
- significant increase in energy
- clearing up the skin

- prevention of nutrient deficiencies

- reduced amount of anti- nutrients and carcinogens in your diet

- improved heart health

- aid with optimal liver function

- prevention of certain cancers

- preventing or treating constipation

Personally, I eat "more raw", or almost fully raw in the summer and during winter I combine raw foods with cooked foods. My rule is: just try to add more raw foods into your diet (even if you don't eat fully raw).

Your body needs enzymes to function and thrive. However, you only have about thirty to thirty- five years' worth of enzymes that your body can manufacture. Once your body start to run out of enzymes, it starts to pillage them from vital organs, leading them to lose their function. This is a very simple explanation of the process, but it directly confronts that greatest issue of enzyme loss. To combat this serious health problem, you should consume about at least sixty percent more raw foods with each meal. Easy! And, as you can see, it's not that much about perfection. It's about balance.

Other Unique Benefits of Eating Raw Foods

- Eating raw foods will get you back in the kitchen. With hundreds of chain restaurants, fast food joints, and instant pre- made meals available, many people are losing the art of good home cooking to processed and refined foods. It is nearly impossible to find a raw food restaurant or even raw options on a menu. After all, no one wants to eat garden salads every time they dine out with friends. Going raw will get you back in the grocery store, exploring new options, and experimenting with unique recipes. Eating home cooked meals will save you money, give you more energy, and encourage you to eat better ingredients.

- Raw food diets are so intense with cleansing your body, that they help you discover underlying food intolerances. Sometimes, our bodies are just not meant to break down and digest certain foods. Many people who have to eat gluten-free products know this struggle first hand. Food intolerances can lead to severe abdominal pain, bloating, and a full night of restless sleep. Raw food diets automatically make you avoid consuming eggs, wheat, dairy, soy, and sugar. When you begin to reintroduce certain ingredients back into your diet, the way your stomach reacts will tell you if you have a food intolerance.

- Going on a raw food diet will make you more intuitive about other parts of your life. Eating clean does wonders for your mental state. People who have done cleanses and detoxes will tell you they experienced incredible mental clarity, hyper- awareness, and focus after the cleanse. When you cut out all of the processed junk your body is used to eating, you will feel more intuitive about what choices are right or wrong in most other aspects of your life. There will no longer be a mental haziness hanging over you, and you will become more conscious of the on- goings in the world around you. You will notice little things that were miniscule detailed before and enjoy the smaller and beautiful things in life.

- Your taste buds will change because of your detox from processed, sugary junk. When you do not drink coffee every morning and avoid your usual night cap before bed, your tastes and preferences will begin to change. You will stop craving your morning coffee, no longer feel the need to finish the day with a glass of alcohol at night, and lose all cravings for a greasy, questionable fast food burger. Sugar cravings will be replaced by more savory temptations, which will only encourage your healthy eating habits and keep you from going down the road of processed carbohydrates.

Chapter 2: The Power of Superfoods

With all the fad diets and recent developments in the food industry, you have probably heard the term "superfood" at some point. A superfood is a food that is especially rich in nutrients, making it exceptionally beneficial for your health. Superfoods may help you lose weight, increase your energy level, nourish your skin and hair, and so much more. While not every smoothie you sip is made up of superfoods, the typical and not-so-typical ingredients have benefits of their own.

Most people tend to have a slight deficiency in one or more vitamins, which can lead to a slew of health problems. From impaired eyesight, bone and muscle aches and pains to fatigue, headaches, and other potentially serious conditions, a deficiency in essential nutrients can have a significant impact on your health and well-being. Fortunately, Mother Nature provides us with fruits and vegetables that are full of all the good stuff your body needs to function. Certain fruits and vegetables are packed with specific nutrients that will restore your vitamin deficiency. Take a look at the following list of the most popular superfoods and healthy ingredients that you use to enhance your smoothies!

<u>Almonds-</u> Almonds taste delicious and keep your skin looking clean and clear. A one-ounce serving contains more than three grams of fiber, potassium, vitamin E, iron, calcium, and magnesium.

<u>Avocado-</u> This green alkaline superfood is fast becoming a superstar in the food industry. From dips to smoothies, avocados are a delicious addition to any meal. Avocados have nearly twenty vitamins, phytonutrients, and minerals in just a one- ounce serving. They are also packed with fiber, folic acid, iron, potassium, magnesium, vitamin B1, B2, B3, B5, B6, vitamin C, vitamin E, and vitamin K. That is a lot of superpower for one food.

<u>Beets-</u> This superfood vegetable has enough vitamins, antioxidants, and nutrients to fight disease and strengthen your vital organs. It has also been suggested by multiple studies that beets can help thwart cancer and similar degenerative diseases.

<u>Blueberries-</u> Blueberries can make any smoothie pop with their fun color and sweet taste. But these small berries also have fiber,

vitamin C, and cancer- fighting elements. Some studies even suggest that eating blueberries can also improve your memory.

Chia seeds- Chia seeds have become popular additions to coffee, smoothies, and even cakes and desserts. These tiny seeds absorb whatever liquid they are soaked in, growing to double their original size. Chia seeds are packed with essential fatty acids, iron, potassium, magnesium, and calcium.

Cranberries- Cranberries are an essential for any holiday feast. This tart little fruit can be cooked, eaten fresh, juiced, or eaten right out of a can. They contain a handful of disease- fighting elements and health benefits. These berries can fight bacteria, inflammation, and heart disease, improve oral health, prevent yeast infections, and prevent ulcers. They are also believed to inhibit the growth of cancer cells.

Garlic- Garlic may make your breath smell a little less-than-desirable, however, they do pack enough disease fighting elements to have been used as an ancient remedy for many years. In modern medicine, garlic has been used to treat high blood pressure, some types of cancer, and even heart disease. In addition, garlic cloves are used to treat yeast infections in women and prostate problem in men.

Ginger- Ginger is fast becoming one of the most internationally recognized superfoods out there. Although it is slightly spicy, ginger has been used as a natural remedy for centuries, as well as a tasty flavor enhancer. Ginger can soothe an upset stomach and reduce inflammation.

Green Tea- Green tea is a popular superfood, found in most cafés and even desserts. Drinking green tea is an ancient health secret that has been used as a natural remedy for centuries. The secret component of green tea is the antioxidants. Green tea contains epigallocatechin gallate (EGCG), a phytochemical that can prevent the growth of cancerous cells. It also contains zinc, selenium, and chromium.

Kale- Kale has become a popular addition to salads and smoothies in the last few years. The tough green leaves blend well with almost any ingredient and also contain fiber, calcium, and iron.

Lemon- Lemon water is known to help aid the detox process, help your digestive system, and increase weight loss. Lemons and limes contain antioxidants and anti- cancer components. These citrus fruits also have a significant amount of vitamin C, which neutralizes free radicals in and outside of your body. This process helps repair damaged cells, reduce inflammation, heal blood vessels, and improve cholesterol. Lemons and limes also reduce the symptoms of osteoarthritis and rheumatoid arthritis, as well as prevent the development of diabetic heart disease.

Peppers- This spicy vegetable is more than just a hot addition to salsas and salads. Bell peppers are packed with more nutrients than you know. Including: vitamin C, vitamin B6, vitamin B2, vitamin B3, vitamin 1, vitamin A, folate, vitamin E, fiber, pantothenic acid, potassium, vitamin K, manganese, magnesium, and phosphorus.

Pistachios- Pistachios have made a name for themselves in the last few years. These little green nuts are filled with fiber and protein. They are also cholesterol- free and contain more potassium than a small banana in just a one- ounce serving.

Pumpkin- Pumpkin is known as a seasonal ingredient for autumn delights, but this superfood has more than just a yummy taste. This orange superfood contains beta- carotene, a pro-vitamin that your body concerts to vitamin A. Vitamin A boosts your immune system and plays an essential role in eye health.

Strawberries- Strawberries are one of the most delicious fruits and one of the most effective superfoods. One cup of strawberries satisfies the daily requirement for vitamin C (which is 74 milligrams for women and 90 milligrams for men per day). Vitamin C boosts your immune system, helps your body repair cells and tissue, and promotes healthy eye function.

Spinach- Spinach is high in antioxidants, anti-inflammatories, and vitamins that keep your eyes and bones healthy. One cup of spinach also contains calcium and vitamin K, which promotes strong bones. It's super alkaline as well (and so are other green veggies and leafy veggies).

Tomatoes- Tomatoes make a great bonus to any sandwich or salad, but they are also a delicious ingredient for savory smoothies. Tomatoes do not have cholesterol, but they do contain omega 3 fatty acids, omega 6 fatty acids, manganese, zinc, copper, zinc, potassium, phosphorus, magnesium, iron, and calcium.

Quinoa- Quinoa are tiny grains that have similar texture to couscous. Although the grains are small, they provide all nine essential amino acids that your body cannot produce by itself. It also contains eight grams of protein per one- cup serving.

Oatmeal- Oatmeal is typically known as a breakfast option, but it can also be used as a main component of your smoothies. Oatmeal is high in fiber, antioxidants, potassium, iron, vitamin B, magnesium, and vitamin A. It also helps to lower cholesterol, ease your digestive system, and improve your metabolism.

<u>Watermelon</u>- Watermelon is summer's most popular fruit, and it packs a day's worth of vitamins A and C in a serving. Watermelon is also speculated to lower blood pressure and reduce the risk of cardiovascular disease. And the lycopene in the fruit can also protect your skin against UV rays.

Chapter 3: 15 Delicious Breakfast Smoothies

Smoothies are one of the easiest things that you can make in the kitchen. All you need to do is pour the ingredients into a blender and pulse until you have a smooth, refreshing beverage. Before you throw everything together, you should really start with only a few of the ingredients, and then pulse them for about five seconds in the blender. Do this for about one minute before adding in the rest of the ingredients and pulsing until you achieve a smooth consistency. Finally, finish your smoothie off with a few ice cubes, blending the ice to chill the beverage.

As the saying goes, breakfast is the most important meal of the day. The more nutritious and filling your breakfast is, the more likely you are to eat healthy throughout the day. Breakfast should provide you with enough vitamins and nutrients to keep you full, energized, and ready to attack the day. Check out these delicious breakfast smoothies guaranteed to start your day right.

Recipe Measurements

I love keeping ingredient measurements as simple as possible- this is why I stick to tablespoons, teaspoons and cups.

The cup measurement I use is the American cup measurement. I also use it for dry ingredients. If you are new to it, let me help you:

If you don't have American Cup measures, just use a metric or imperial liquid measuring jug and fill your jug with your ingredient to the corresponding level. Here's how to go about it:

1 American Cup= 250ml= 8 fl.oz

For example:

If a recipe calls for 1 cup of almonds, simply place your almonds into your measuring jug until it reaches the 250 ml/8oz mark.

I know that different countries use different measurements and I wanted to make things simple for you.

Wake- Up Green Smoothie- 1 Serving

Ingredients

- 2 Limes, Halved and Peeled
- 1 Cup of Raw Coconut Meat
- 1 Avocado, Peeled and Pitted
- 1 tsp. of Grated Limed Zest
- 2 Ice Cubes
- 1 Pinch of Sea Salt
- 2 Cups of Baby Spinach
- ½ Tbs. of Coconut Oil
- ½ Cucumber, Chopped
- ¾ Cup of Coconut Water

Blend and enjoy!

Grapefruit Immune Booster- 1 Serving

Ingredients

- 1 Cup of Coconut Milk
- 1 Grapefruit, Juiced
- 1 Cup of Baby Spinach

Blend and enjoy!

Peachy Green Smoothie- 2 Servings

Ingredients

- 1 Peach, Chopped
- 1 Cup of Baby Spinach
- 1 Cup of Coconut Water
- 1 Banana, Sliced

Blend and enjoy!

Tahitian Coconut Blast- 1 Serving

Ingredients

- 1 ½ Cup of Pineapple, Chopped
- 1 Ice Cube
- 1 Tbs. of Coconut Flakes
- ¼ Cup of Coconut Water
- 1 Cup of Baby Spinach
- ¾ Cup of Almond Milk

Blend and enjoy!

Banana and Blueberry Smoothie- 1 Serving

Ingredients

- 1 Banana
- ½ Bag of Frozen Blueberries
- ½ Cup of Kale
- 1 Tbs. of Hemp Seeds
- 1 Cup of Coconut Water
- 2 Tbs. of Wheatgrass Juice

Blend and enjoy!

Kiwi Melon Power Blend- 1 Serving

Ingredients

- 1 Cup of Melon
- 4 Kiwis, Peeled and Chopped
- 4 Mint Leaves
- 1 tsp. of Wheatgrass Juice

Blend and enjoy!

Apple and Avocado Energy Smoothie- 1 Serving

Ingredients

- ½ Avocado
- ½ Apple, Partially Peeled
- 1/3 Cup of Almond Milk
- ¼ Cup of Water
- 1 Cup of Ice

Blend and enjoy!

Strawberries and Cream Smoothie- 1 Serving

Ingredients

- 1 Cup of Frozen Strawberries
- 1 Cup of Almond Milk
- 2 tsp. of Flaxseed Oil

Blend and enjoy!

Apple Berry Smoothie- 1 Serving

Ingredients

- 1 ½ Tbs. of Chia Seeds
- ½ Cup of Frozen Mixed Berries
- 1 Ice Cube
- ½ an Apple, Peeled and Chopped
- 8 Oz. of Water
- 1 Tbs. of Flaxseed Oil

Blend and enjoy!

Citrus Kale Breakfast Blend- 1 Serving

Ingredients

- 1 ½ Cup of Kale, Chopped
- 1 Orange, Peeled and Deseeded
- ½ Tbs. of Chia Seeds
- ¼ Lime, Peeled
- 1 Banana, Peeled and Sliced
- 1/3 Cup of Coconut Milk

Blend and enjoy!

Orange Mango Breakfast Delight- 2 Servings

Ingredients

- 1 ½ Cup of Orange Juice
- ½ tsp. of Lime Zest
- ½ Cup of Coconut Water
- 2 Cups of Frozen Mango
- ½ an Avocado, Peeled and Pitted

Blend and enjoy!

Cucumber Grapefruit Smoothie- 1 Serving

Ingredients

- 1/3 Cup of Grapefruit Juice, Chilled
- ½ Cucumber, Peeled and Sliced
- 4 Ice Cubes
- 1 Peeled Apple, Cored and Sliced
- ½ Raw Beet, Peeled and Chopped

Blend and enjoy!

Spinach Berry Smoothie- 1 Serving

Ingredients

- 1 Cup of Baby Spinach
- 1 Tbs. of Coconut Oil
- 1 Cup of Almond Milk
- 1 Cup of Mixed Frozen Berries
- 1 Tbs. of Cacao Powder
- 5 Ice Cubes
- 1 Tbs. of Vegan Maple Syrup
- 1 Tbs. of Almond Butter

Blend and enjoy!

Pomegranate and Chai Energy Smoothie- 1 Serving

Ingredients

- 1 Tbs. of Chia Seeds
- 1 Cup of Pomegranate Seeds
- 1 Cup of Kale Leaves
- ½ Cup of Coconut Milk
- 4 Ice Cubes

Blend and enjoy!

Honeydew and Almond Smoothie- 2 Servings

Ingredients

- 2 Cup of Honeydew, Diced
- 1 ½ Cup of Ice
- 2 Cups of Almond Milk
- ½ Cup of Almonds
- 1 Tbs. of Ground Flaxseed

Blend and enjoy!

Chapter 4: Savory Meal Replacement Smoothies

What you eat throughout the day determines your weight loss success, as well are your mental state and physical wellbeing. The food you eat effects your body; it can either weigh you down and make you feel lethargic, or energize your body and boost your mood and inspire positivity. Many people make the mistake of eating too much during the day.

Negative eating habits, like snacking or overflowing your plate at dinner, can significantly impact your health, cause future ailments, and make you less productive during the day. Smoothies are the perfect combination of healthy and filling. The sugar and fiber that superfoods contain will keep you going way past your usual midday energy lull and stop future temptations of bingeing on a box of cookies. And the additional nutrients and vitamins will help your body heal and enhance your immune system. Not to mention the fact that smoothies are really easy for your body to digest. When you drink a smoothie, you are giving your vital organs a break from processing tough foods, like meat and starch.

Savory Meal Replacement Smoothies

When most people think of smoothies, they picture a variety of fruit blended together. However, after reading chapter two, you now know that there are plenty of vegetables that you can add into the mixture as well. If you are not the biggest fan of kale or spinach, you do not have to sacrifice being healthy to have a tasty smoothie. You can use almost any of your favorite vegetable in your meal replacement smoothies; making them a savory meal instead of a sweet treat. This chapter contains twenty- two delicious and savory meal replacement smoothies that you can consume in place of your typical eating habits. Check out the following smoothies, choose your favorites, and enjoy!

Refreshing Mint Green Smoothies- 1 Serving

Ingredients

- 1 Avocado, Peeled and Pitted
- ½ Cup of Kale
- ½ Cucumber, Peeled and Sliced
- 1 Cup of Almond Milk
- Fresh Juice from 1 Lemon
- ¼ Cup of Mint Leaves
- 1 Pinch of Cinnamon

Blend and enjoy!

Savory Italian Blend-1 Serving

Ingredients

- ½ Cucumber, Peeled and Sliced
- ¼ Cup of Rosemary Infusion, Chilled
- 2 Tomatoes, Peeled and Sliced
- 1 Tbs. Extra Virgin Olive Oil
- ½ Clove of Garlic
- ½ Cup of Kale, Juiced
- ¼ Cup of Onion, Chopped

- Fresh Juice of 1 Lemon
- Small Pinch of Black Pepper
- Small Pinch of Himalaya Salt

Blend and enjoy!

Ginger and Cucumber Smoothie- 1 Serving

Ingredients

- ½ Avocado, Peeled and Pitted
- ½ Cucumber, Peeled and Sliced
- 2 Cups of Baby Spinach
- 1 Stem of Fresh Parsley
- ½ Cup of Coconut Water
- Fresh Juice of 1 Lemon
- 2 Stems of Fresh Mint
- 2 Ice Cubes
- 1" Piece of Fresh Ginger

Blend and enjoy!

Red and Green Veggie Blend- 1 Serving

Ingredients

- 1 Cucumber, Peeled and Sliced
- ½ Red Pepper
- ½ Avocado, Peeled and Pitted
- 1 Lime, Peeled
- 1 Cup of Baby Spinach
- 2 Tomatoes, Peeled and Sliced
- ½ Cup of Coconut Milk

Blend and enjoy!

Dandelion Detox- 2 Serving

Ingredients

- 1 Lemon, Peeled
- 1 Banana, Peeled and Sliced
- 1 Bunch of Dandelion Greens
- 2 Apples, Peeled and Sliced
- 2 tsp. of Flaxseeds
- ¾ Cup of Coconut Water

Blend and enjoy!

Green Ginger Smoothie- 1 Serving

Ingredients

- 1 Avocado, Peeled and Pitted
- 1" of Fresh Garlic
- 1 Bunch of Carrots, with some of its Greens
- ½ Lemon, Peeled
- 1/3 Cup of Water
- Small Pinch of Sea Salt
- Small Pinch of Black Pepper

Blend and enjoy!

Raspberry Tea Smoothie- 2 Servings

Ingredients

- 1 Cup of Frozen Blueberries
- 3 Cups of Baby Spinach
- 1 Banana, Peeled and Sliced
- ½ tsp. of Cinnamon
- 10 Oz. of Raspberry-Hibiscus Tea, Chilled

Blend and enjoy!

Apple Beet Sweet Blend- 1 Serving

Ingredients

- 1 Apple, Peeled and Sliced
- 1 Cup of Cherries, without Pits
- 2 Cups of Kale, Chopped
- ½ Cup of Beets, Chopped
- ½ Cup of Pineapple
- 8 Oz. of Coconut Milk

Blend and enjoy!

Soothing Watermelon Smoothie- 2 Servings

Ingredients

- 1 Frozen Banana, Peeled and Sliced
- 2 Cups of Watermelon
- 5 Fresh Mint Leaves
- 6 Strawberries

Blend and enjoy!

Carrot and Turmeric Detox – 1 Serving

Ingredients

- 1 Orange, Peeled and Deseeded
- 1 Carrot, Peeled and Chopped
- 1 Banana, Peeled and Sliced
- ¼ Lemon, Peeled
- ¼ tsp. of Ground Turmeric
- 1 Handful of Baby Spinach
- 1" Piece of Fresh Ginger
- 8 Oz. of Almond Milk

Blend and enjoy!

Cantaloupe Meal Replacement Smoothie- 2 Servings

Ingredients

- 3 Figs
- 1 Mango, Peeled and Pitted
- 2 Cups of Cantaloupe
- 2 Cups of Baby Spinach
- 6 Oz. of Coconut Water
- ½ tsp. of Ground Cinnamon

Blend and enjoy!

Banana and Fig Smoothie- 2 Servings

Ingredients

- 3 Figs
- 6 Oz. of Almond Water
- 2 Bananas
- 1 Peach, Peeled
- ½ Cup of Baby Spinach
  Blend and enjoy!

Grape and Orange Juice Smoothie- 1 Serving

Ingredients

- 1 Orange, Peeled and Sliced
- 2 Stalks of Celery, Chopped
- 1 Cup of Red Grapes
- ½ Cup of Coconut Water
- 1 Pear, Peeled and Sliced
- 2 Cups of Kale

Blend and enjoy!

Mango Grape Energy Blend- 2 Servings

Ingredients

- 1 Mango, Peeled and Sliced
- 1 Tomato
- 2 Cups of Red Grapes
- ½ Cup of Water
- 2 Cups of Baby Spinach

Blend and enjoy!

Green Plum Smoothie- 2 Servings

Ingredients

- 2 Cups of Watermelon
- 2 Celery Stalks, Chopped
- ½ Cup of Coconut Water
- 2 Plums, Deseeded
- 2 Cups of Kale
- 1 Banana, Peeled and Sliced

Blend and enjoy!

Chocolate Zucchini Smoothie- 2 Servings

Ingredients

- ¼ Cup of Peanuts, Chopped
- 2 Frozen Bananas, Peeled and Sliced
- 1 Cup of Almond Milk
- 1 Cup of Frozen Zucchini, Grated

Blend and enjoy!

Yam and Banana Smoothie- 2 Servings

Ingredients

- 1 Cup of Almond Milk
- 2 Yams, Cooked, Cooled Down, Peeled and Sliced
- 2 Cups of Ice Cubes
- 1 Banana, Peeled and Sliced

Directions:

1. Place all of the ingredients into the blender and, and blend until smooth and creamy. Enjoy!

Sweet Potato Almond Smoothie- 1 Serving

Ingredients

- 1 Sweet Potato, peeled, sliced, cooked and cooled down
- 2 Cups of Almond Milk
- ¼ tsp. of Ground Cinnamon
- 3 Tsp. of Cashews
- 1 Banana, Peeled and Sliced

Blend and enjoy!

Broccoli and Cucumber Lunch Blend- 1 Serving

Ingredients

- 2 Cups of Broccoli, Chopped
- ½ Cup of Water
- 1 Cup of Green Grapes, Seedless
- 1 Lime, Juice
- 1 Cucumber, Peeled and Sliced

Blend and enjoy!

Cabbage and Peach Smoothie- 1 Serving

Ingredients

- ¾ Cup of Cabbage, Chopped
- ¼ Cup of Ice Cubed
- 1 Cup of Red Grapes, Seedless
- 1 Carrot, Peeled and Chopped
- ¼ Cup of Water
- 1 Cup of Frozen Peaches, Sliced

Blend and enjoy!

Green Spinach and Jalapeno Lunch Smoothie- 1 Serving

Ingredients

- ½ tsp. of Jalapeno Pepper, Chopped
- 2 Bananas, Peeled and Sliced
- 1 Cup of Frozen Mango
- 1 Cup of Water
- 2 Cups of Baby Spinach

Blend and enjoy!

Cranberry Rhubarb Smoothie- 1 Serving

Ingredients

- 1 Frozen Banana, Peeled and Sliced
- 1 Cup of Cranberry Juice, Chilled
- 1 Cup of Frozen Rhubarb, Chopped
- 1 tsp. of Vanilla Extract
- 1 Tbs. of Chia Seeds

Blend and enjoy!

Chapter 5: 14 Sweet Dessert Smoothies

Banana Almond Smoothie- 1 Serving

Ingredients

- 1 Frozen Banana, Peeled and Sliced
- 1 Tbs. of Ground Flaxseed
- 5 Oz. of Almond Milk
- 2" of Vanilla Bean -or- 1 tsp. of Vanilla Extract
- 3 Swiss Chard Leaves
- ¼ of an Avocado, Sliced

Blend and enjoy!

Gingerbread Dessert Smoothie- 2 Servings

Ingredients

- ½ tsp. of Ground Cinnamon
- 1 Cup of Almond Milk
- 1 tsp. of Molasses
- 2 Frozen Bananas, Peeled and Sliced
- 1 tsp. of Vanilla Extract
- 1 ½ tsp. of Fresh Ginger, Grated

Blend and enjoy!

Vegan Pumpkin Pie Dessert Smoothie- 1 Serving

Ingredients

- 2 Cups of Baby Spinach
- ½ Cup of Pure Canned Pumpkin
- 10 Oz. of Almond Milk
- ½ tsp. of Cinnamon
- 1 Cup of Mango
- ½ tsp. of Vanilla Extract
- 3 Tbs. of Cashews

Blend and enjoy!

Orange Chocolate Delight- 1 Serving

Ingredients

- 1 Frozen Banana, Peeled and Sliced
- 1 Tbs. of Cacao Powder
- 2 Cups of Baby Spinach
- 1 ½ Oranges, Peeled and Deseeded
- 2 Oz. of Coconut Water
- 2 Tsp. of Cashews
  Blend and enjoy!

Strawberry and Almond Smoothie- 1 Serving

Ingredients

- 12 Frozen Strawberries
- 4 Tbs. of Chia Seeds
- ½ Cup of Goji Berries
- 2 tsp. of Vanilla Extract
- ¼ Cup of Almonds
- 6 Oz. of Almond Milk

Blend and enjoy!

Banana Tropical Smoothie- 2 Servings

Ingredients

- 1 Orange, Peeled and Deseeded
- 1 Cup of Almond Milk
- 1 Frozen Banana, Peeled and Sliced
- ½ tsp. of Vanilla Extract
- 1 tsp. of Vegan Maple Syrup

Blend and enjoy!

Banana Peanut Butter Dessert Smoothie- 1 Serving

Ingredients

- 1 Frozen Banana, Peeled and Sliced
- 2 Tbs. of Vegan Cocoa Powder
- 1 Cup of Almond Milk
- 1 Tbs. of All- Natural Peanut Butter

Blend and enjoy!

Chocolate Cappuccino Smoothie- 1 Serving

Ingredients

- 1 Frozen Banana, Peeled and Sliced
- 1 Tbs. of Vegan Maple Syrup
- 1 Cup of De-Caffeinated Coffee
- 1 Tbs. of Vegan Cocoa Powder

Blend and enjoy!

Cherry Coconut Ice Smoothie- 3 Servings

Ingredients

- 14 Oz. of Organic Full- Fat Coconut Milk
- 2/3 Cup of Water
- 2 Cups of Cherries, Pitted
- The Juice of ½ a Lemon
- ½ Avocado, Peeled and Pitted
- 1/3 Cup of Cashews, Soaked for 20 Minutes, then Drained
- 10 Dried Dates, Pitted
- 2 Tbs. of Vegan Chocolate, Finely Chopped
- 2 Ice Cubes

Blend and enjoy!

Coconut Chia Dessert Smoothie- 4 Servings

Ingredients

- ¼ Cup of Chia Seeds
- ½ tsp. of Vanilla Extract
- 1 tsp. Ground Cinnamon
- 1 Date, Pitted
- 1 Cup of Coconut Milk

- ½ Cup of Blueberries
- 1 Cup of Vegan Yogurt
- 1 tsp. of Ground Flaxseed
- 1 Fig
- 1 tsp. of Sesame Seeds

Blend and enjoy!

Raspberry Fig Smoothie- 2 Servings

Ingredients

- 1 Cup of Frozen Raspberries
- 1 Tbs. of Vegan Maple Syrup
- ½ Cup of Cashews
- 1 Cups of Almond Milk, Chilled
- 2 Tbs. of Cacao Powder
- 2 Fresh Figs
- ½ tsp. of Sweet Paprika

Blend and enjoy!

Sunbutter and Date Smoothie- 1 Serving

Ingredients

- 2 Cups of Spinach
- 1 Cup of Almond Milk
- 2 Dates, Pitted
- 2 Tbs. of Sunbutter
- 2 Ice Cubes
- 1 Frozen Apple, Sliced
- 1/8 tsp. of Ground Cinnamon

- ¼ tsp. of Vanilla Extract

Blend and enjoy!

Chocolate Banana Dessert Smoothie- 1 Serving

Ingredients

- 1 Cup of Frozen Kale Leaves
- 1 ½ Frozen Bananas, Peeled and Sliced
- 1 ½ Cups of Almond Milk
- 2 Tbs. of Cocoa Powder
- 2 Dates, Pitted
- 1/8 tsp. of Ground Cinnamon
- 2 Tbs. of Hulled Hemp Seeds
- ¼ of an Avocado, Peeled and Pitted
- 2 Ice Cubes

Blend and enjoy!

Coffee and Cocoa Sweet Blend Not So Alkaline Treat- 2 Servings

Ingredients

- 1 Cup of Decaffeinated Coffee, Chilled to Room Temperature
- 2 Tbs. of Cocoa Powder
- ½ tsp. of Vanilla Extract
- ¼ Cup of Almond Milk
- 8 Ice Cubes
- 3 Dates, Pitted
- 1 Cup of Spinach

Blend and enjoy!

Sweet Dessert Smoothies

Chapter 6: Creative and Unique Smoothie Ideas

Vanilla Hazelnut Smoothie- 1 Serving

Ingredients

- ¾ Cup of Hazelnuts
- 3 Cups of Water
- 1 Vanilla Bean, Chopped
- ¼ Cup of Almonds
- ½ tsp. of Cinnamon
- 2 Dates, Pitted

Directions:

1. Place the hazelnuts and almonds in a bowl filled with water. Soak the nuts overnight, between eight to twelve hours.

2. Rinse and drain the nuts. Then, place them in a blender with the rest of the ingredients and blend on high until all of the components are completely integrated.

3. Once the smoothie is blended, use a nut milk bag over a large bowl, and pour the smoothie into the bag. Squeeze the bottom of the bag to release the liquid, leaving the excess nut pulp in the bag

Butternut Squash and Ginger Smoothie- 2 Servings

Ingredients

- 1 Cup (Packed) of Roasted Butternut Squash
- 1 Tbs. of Chia Seeds
- 1 ½ Cup of Almond Milk
- ½ tsp. of Ground Ginger
- 1 ½ tsp. of Vanilla Extract
- 3 Dates, Pitted
- 2 tsp. of Cinnamon
- 2 Ice Cubes

Directions:

1. Before making the smoothie, you must prepare the butternut squash. Start by preheating your oven to 400 Degrees. Then, prepare a baking sheet with parchment paper.

2. Next, slice the stem off the squash, and then slice the vegetable in half lengthwise. Then, scoop out the seeds with a spoon and lightly coat the squash with olive oil and a sprinkle of salt.

3. Place the butternut squash onto the baking sheet, with the cut side facing up. Roast in the oven for 45 minutes, until the vegetable is tender with a fork and golden brown on the bottom.

4. Remove the squash from the oven and allow to. Once the veggie has cooled down, you can blend together all of the ingredients into a smoothie and enjoy!

Creative and Unique Smoothie Ideas

Sweet Chocolatey Cake Batter Dessert Smoothie- 1 Serving

Ingredients

- 1 Frozen Banana, Peeled and Sliced
- 1 Cup of Almond Milk
- 1 Tbs. of Almond Butter
- 1/3 Cup of Oats
- 1 tsp. of Cinnamon
- 2 Ice Cubes
- 1 tsp. of Vanilla Extract
- 2 Tbs. of Vegan Chocolate Chips

Directions:

1. Mix together the almond milk and oats in a mixing bowl. Place the oats into the refrigerator and let them soak for approximately one hour.

2. After soaking the oats, place them into a blender with the rest of the ingredients (besides the chocolate chips).

3. Blend the ingredients on high setting until the mixture is smooth. Next, add in the chocolate chips and blend on low setting until the smoothie is slightly chunky. Enjoy!

Peppermint and Hemp Blend- 1 Serving

Ingredients

- 1 Frozen Banana, Peeled and Sliced
- ½ Cup of Boiling Water
- 1 Peppermint Tea Bag
- 2 Tbs. of Hemp Hearts
- 2 Cups of Spinach
- 5 Ice Cubes
- ½ Cup of Almond Milk
- 3 Tbs. of Vegan Chocolate Chips, Divided

Directions:

1. Steep the peppermint tea bag in the boiling water until you are ready to add it into the smoothie. Wait until the water has cooled to room temperature. This should take about thirty minutes.

2. Next, place all of the ingredients (except the chocolate chips) into the blender. Blend the ingredients together until smooth.

3. Pour half of the chocolate chips into the blender and quickly pulse. Pour the smoothie into a glass, top it off with the rest of the chocolate chips, and enjoy!

Blueberry Chai Smoothie- 1 Serving

Ingredients

- 2 Tbs. of Gluten Free Oats
- 1 ½ Cup of Almond Milk
- 1 tsp. of Vanilla Extract
- ½ Cup of Blueberries
- 1 Tbs. of Vegan Vanilla Protein Powder (Optional)
- 1 Tbs. of Chia Seeds

Directions:

1. The night before you want to drink this smoothie, begin preparing the ingredients. Start by combining the ingredients (except for the blueberries) in a container. Stir the mixture together and place in the refrigerator. Allow the ingredients to sit overnight.

2. After the smoothie ingredients are done soaking, pour them into a blender with the blueberries. Blend the mixture until smooth. Enjoy!

Lemon Raspberry Poppy Seed Smoothie- 1 Serving

Ingredients

- 1 Tbs. of Almond Butter
- 1 1.2 Cup of Almond Milk
- 1 Tbs. of Lemon Juice
- 1 Tbs. of Chia Seeds
- ½ Cup of Raspberries
- 1 tsp. of Vanilla Extract
- 1 ½ tsp. of Poppy Seeds
- 2 Tbs. of Gluten Free Oats
- The Zest of 1 Lemon

Directions:

1. The night before you want to make your smoothie, combine all of the ingredients in a class container. Place the container into your refrigerator overnight.
2. When the ingredients are finished soaking, add them into the blender and combine until smooth.

Banana Bread Smoothie- 1 Serving

Ingredients

- 1 ¼ Cups of Almond Milk
- 1 Tbs. of Raisins
- ½ tsp. of Cinnamon
- 1 Frozen Banana, Peeled and Sliced
- ½ tsp. of Vanilla Extracts
- 2 Tbs. of Gluten Free Oats
- 1 Tbs. of Walnuts

Directions:

1. The night before, combine the ingredients in a plastic container (excluding the banana and ¼ cup of almond milk). Stir together and place in the refrigerator.

2. In the morning, pour the contents of the container into your blender, adding in the banana and left over almond milk.

3. Blend until smooth and enjoy!

Sleepy Time Tea Smoothie- 1 Serving

Ingredients

- 12 Cup of Strawberries
- 1 Cup of Almond Milk
- 1 Tbs. of Dried Chamomile Flowers
- ¼ Cup of Gluten Free Quinoa, Cooked

Directions:

1. Steep the chamomile flowers in boiling water for approximately five minutes. Then, refrigerate the tea until it has cooled down.

2. Once you are ready to make your smoothie, combine the ingredients into a blender using half a cup of the chamomile tea.

3. Blend until smooth and enjoy!

Make Your Own Unique Smoothies with This Guide!

Step 1: Pick Your Main and Supporting Fruit or Vegetable (Choose 2 or 3 from this list)

- Avocado

- Apple

- Apricot

- Banana

- Blueberry

- Blackberry

- Beets

- Broccoli

-Carrots

- Cabbage

- Celery

-Cantaloupes

- Cherries

Make Your Own Unique Smoothies with This Guide!

-Cranberries

-Cucumbers

-Collards

- Figs

- Grapes

- Grapefruit

- Guava

- Honeydew

- Kale

- Kiwi

- Kumquat

- Lime

- Lemon

- Lychees

- Lettuce

- Mango

- Nectarine

- Melon

- Oranges

Make Your Own Unique Smoothies with This Guide!

- Peppers

- Pumpkin

- Passionfruit

- Peach

- Pear

- Papaya

- Raspberry

- Pomegranate

- Pineapple

- Rhubarb

- Strawberry

- Spinach

- Sweet Potato

- Squash

- Tangerine

-Tomato

- Zucchini

- Watermelon

Step 2: Pick Your Fiber and Thickening Ingredients (Choose Up to 2 Foods from this List)

- Instant Gluten Free Oats

- Almonds

- Coconut Oil

- Macadamia Nuts

- Cashews

- Pecans

- Pistachios

- Nut Butters

- Desiccated Coconut

- Silken Tofu

Step 3: Pick Your Smoothie Thinners (Choose 1 or 2 from this List)

- Water

- Coconut Water

- Almond Milk

- Cashew Milk

- Oat Milk

- Quinoa Milk

- Coconut Milk

- Rice Milk

-Soy Milk

Step 4: Pick Your Extra Nutrients for Health and Wellness (Choose up to 2 from this list)

- Green Tea Powder

- Chia Seeds

- Plant Protein Powder

- Maca Powder

- Cacao Nibs

- Cacao Powder

- Cayenne Pepper

- Turmeric

- Fresh Ginger

- Acai Berry Powder

Step 5: Pick Your Flavoring Ingredients (Choose 1 from this List)

- Cinnamon

- Chai Spice Powder

- Cardamom

- Herbs

-Lemon Juice

- Cocoa Powder

- Pumpkin Spice Powder

- Lime Juice

- Nutmeg

Step 6: Pick Your Sweeteners (Optional)

- Vegan Maple Syrup

- Dried Figs

- Dates

- Vanilla Extract

- Rice Malt Syrup

Step 7: Pick Your Toppings (Optional)

- Fruit

- Sunflower Seeds

- Goji Berries

- Coconut Shavings

- Chia Seeds

- Pumpkin Seeds

- Goji Berries

- Cacao Nibs

- Nuts

Make Your Own Unique Smoothies with This Guide!

Don't forget to join our free vegan newsletter for more inspiration!

You Will Get Free Instant Access to This Complimentary PDF eBook

Insanely good + super healthy, 100% vegan smoothies with secret ingredients…YUM…

Just follow the link below:

www.yourwellnessbooks.com/karen-smoothies

Problems with your download? Email me:

karenveganbooks@gmail.com

Conclusion

Thank you again for purchasing this book!

I hope this book was able to help you prepare to take on the alkaline lifestyle and live a better, healthier life.

The next step is to start trying out all of the yummy and unique recipes in this book and begin the next chapter of your life as a raw food enthusiast and enjoy all of the health benefits of eating clean.

Finally, if you enjoyed this book, then I'd like to ask you for a favor, would you be kind enough to leave a review for this book on Amazon? It'd be greatly appreciated!

Thank you and good luck!

Sending you lots of love from here

Karen

******

More vegan friendly books by Karen available at:

www.amazon.com/author/karengreenvang

www.ingramcontent.com/pod-product-compliance
Lightning Source LLC
Chambersburg PA
CBHW042118100526
44587CB00025B/4112